GOLDEN HARVEST

Other books of White Eagle's teaching

THE GENTLE BROTHER
HEAL THYSELF
THE LIVING WORD OF ST JOHN
MORNING LIGHT
THE PATH OF THE SOUL
PRAYER IN THE NEW AGE
THE QUIET MIND
SPIRITUAL UNFOLDMENT I
SPIRITUAL UNFOLDMENT II
THE STILL VOICE
SUNRISE
THE WAY OF THE SUN
WISDOM FROM WHITE EAGLE

GOLDEN
HARVEST

How to become
a Centre of Love

WHITE EAGLE

THE WHITE EAGLE PUBLISHING TRUST
LISS · HAMPSHIRE · ENGLAND

First Edition: December 1958
Reprinted: May 1969
Reprinted: December 1974
Reprinted: July 1979
Reprinted: July 1981
Reprinted: July 1987

© *Copyright, The White Eagle Publishing Trust, 1958*

ISBN 0 85487 017 2

Printed in Great Britain
at the University Printing House, Oxford
by David Stanford
Printer to the University

CONTENTS

∽

Foreword

The words of this book were all spoken by White Eagle to students on the path of spiritual unfoldment. He speaks from a higher level of consciousness than we as yet possess, who have only proceeded a little way on the path. His deep compassion and understanding of human need are the result of experience and final conquest of earthly life; and he knows too well the tribulations, great and small, which beset us all as we continue to struggle with our human problems.

He has passed beyond the limitations of our mortality and has witnessed the indescribable happiness of life made perfect. He knows the richness of that spiritual golden harvest which awaits every man and woman who labours faithfully and valorously on earth. Because, like all the wise elder brethren of the human race, he is full of understanding love for humanity, he comes back to tell how men may sow and reap this harvest of happiness in this life as well as in the next.

This book, the third of the present Series, differs somewhat from the preceding two books

—*Morning Light* and *Sunrise*—of which details will be found at the end of this volume. For although it has an unfolding plan which will be readily apparent, it is not intended to be read through from cover to cover continuously and then laid on one side. Each small section is complete in itself, so that when the book is opened at random every page will yield its treasure of wisdom and give its answer to the reader's particular need.

Those who have compiled it have done so in the hope that it may become the reader's constant companion in joy and sorrow alike, guiding and comforting always; and that the practical wisdom that it contains may become a living reality; and above all that the essence of love which poured like a benediction upon the listeners when the messages were spoken, may have found its way into the printed word and thus into the heart of the reader.

The Path of Light

If you look up into the sky on a clear night your small earthly mind becomes dazed by the countless stars and stellar systems which are displayed. Yet you see only the outward aspect of the heavens. Every one of those stars and planets is under the direction of a Great Soul—shall we even say a 'God'?—who watches over its life and activity. Meditate upon the thought of the countless beings existing even in your own solar system who are instruments of God's love; all are proclaiming by their life of service the same truth of love and brotherhood.

Consider a butterfly's wing; for a moment try to imagine its beauty, its delicacy of form, its many colours. Or else take a little wild flower with its jewelled petals and stamens. Then examine either of these under a microscope, and you will be overwhelmed by the wondrous intricacy of composition which will be revealed. Yet these are only infinitesimal aspects of the glories of Creation. Throughout all physical life and ranging out into the higher ethers are indescribable glories waiting for man's discovery.

You have it within your own power to reach those higher planes, when once you have learnt to control and discipline your desires and emotions and so to rise above the limited consciousness of your physical life; to enter into and behold the finer ethers which interpenetrate gross physical matter. The glory of God's Plan of Creation is beyond the capacity of the finite mind to understand, but as you unfold spiritually the limitations fall away, and you are able to enter the heavenly realms, and there see God's plan for your future and for the future of all mankind revealed.

Mastership or Christhood is not only for a selected few; all the children of God have their feet set upon the selfsame path. You are God's child, having within you potential Mastership and Christhood. As part of the great Plan you have been given power of free-will choice, and provided with the exact conditions which you most need for the development of your soul, and the unfoldment of your spirit.

A seed or bulb contains within itself all the beauties that the flower will presently reveal. When planted in the earth, by its very nature it begins to grow and later to flower, and when this happens you say, 'What a miracle is this! Out of that tiny seed has come this glorious flower!' Is this not an illustration of man's real nature and life, his growth from a seed, his flowering into spiritual life? At his beginning his spirit is sown in the heart; it is the seed of the Christ-man he will some day become. During his many incarnations the man will confront the conditions, undergo the experiences, triumph over the difficulties, temptations and weaknesses inseparable from mortal life, in order eventually to develop and bring forth this flowering of the Christ spirit.

If you could hold fast, be constant to this one viewpoint, it would help you so much in your daily life by giving you patience and courage to persevere with the wonderful piece of work that has been entrusted to you.

The Test of Strength

The answer to all your personal and human problems lies in your surrender to the Will of God, in your saying within your heart, 'Thy Will be done, O God!' But this surrender is very difficult for those of you who are just setting out upon the spiritual path, particularly when you think you already know more than in reality you can truly understand or attempt to put into practice.

All who wish to be used in the Master's service have to withstand great pressure and to be well tested. Let us suppose the Master called on you to do some very important piece of work which might affect the well-being of many souls; and suppose you had not been previously tested and well proved? It is possible that you would break down under stress. We are telling you this in order to help you in your endeavours to follow the path of light, with all its attendant testings and disappointments.

We are permitted to point out the way. One thing is very sure, and this is God's enduring love. God is ever with you even though at times He may appear to veil His countenance. Hold fast to belief in His love and wisdom and you will always come through the mists into the light. Rest assured that every time you are tested and manage (with God's strength) to stand up to your testing, you will advance a step further on the path. We would call each of these trials, which are really soul-testings, minor initiations. Initiation is an awakening of the spirit in man; and as a result of that awakening, a continued unfoldment of the Christ power within. It brings about an expansion of consciousness which will reveal the heavenly mysteries. You can listen to many words, read many books; but until you have actually passed one of these soul-testings you will know only with your mind, and not with your whole being; you will not have acquired that knowledge which endures.

The tests or initiations which come to you on the spiritual path fall into four main categories, and are concerned with the spiritual elements of your being. In the first initiation, that of the Water, the soul who passes all the tests becomes an initiate of the Water element; which implies that the emotions are controlled and directed wisely from then onwards. In the next degree the mind learns how to control thought—how to discriminate between the real and the unreal, the false and true, the black and white, the negative and positive, the lower and the higher mind. The candidate learns discernment. That is the Air initiation. The Fire initiation is the discipline and wise use of the power of love; and lastly comes the Earth initiation, when the lower nature is crucified or overcome, and man seeks only to serve God and his brother man. Then we behold the arisen Christ, or the soul that having freed itself is no longer influenced by the carnal or fierce emotional desire-nature of the lower self, or by the dominating mentality which kills—for truly the mind-of-earth can be the slayer of the real. Only when trained and disciplined through contact with the divine Love does man's intellect change into divine intelligence. That is why all great souls become gentle and simple, sweet, childlike, and of goodly intelligence. The arisen Christ is born from the heart, not from the intellect.

Whatever stress or difficulty you are called upon to endure, look up to the heavenly light, be constant to the divine Spirit. You will never regret your faith, your confidence in the power of God not only to bring you through your particular wilderness, but to bless you with understanding of the purpose in your sorrow or tribulation.

Once you have set your feet upon the path, remember you cannot compromise. You must be strict, not with others but with yourself. Things are either right or wrong. When once you have seen this path of self-discipline, purity, loving service, gentleness and perfection revealed, quietly pursue this path. We do not speak of any personal reward; nevertheless, the joy which accrues from this sort of life is beyond all earthly understanding. We do not bid you to mortify the flesh, but rather to glorify the flesh by release of the Christ spirit within, remembering that the flesh also is of God and must become illumined and purified, glorified by the spirit of the Son of God.

Ring True

Many set their feet upon the path believing that

to get anywhere they must learn many occult and magical secrets. But they are eventually disappointed, because the spiritual mysteries can never be conveyed to a soul through words alone.

The real power to perform so-called miracles can only come to you through your working to attain it. You can read every book in the libraries of the world, and know many interesting facts, and still remain impotent. The only way you will learn to work the oracle is through diligent work in your daily life. It is of no avail to dream, and hope, and wish. You must turn up your sleeves and get down to real practical service to humanity. It may be only thoroughly scrubbing a floor, or doing something much more distasteful; it may mean giving humble and sincere service to one to whom you do not feel drawn, or giving your hand to him in brotherhood—perhaps a difficult task. It may mean controlling your own wayward tongue and thoughts, and finding that the world gives you no credit because nobody is aware of the battle which you wage with yourself.

This is the kind of work we mean when we say, 'Turn up your sleeves, get right down on your knees in humility, and scrub the floor of your own lodge or temple.' This also implies having courage when in adversity, and facing apparent injustice with a calm spirit, secure in the knowledge that God in His love has led you to face injustice for a wise purpose.

Be true. This is the essence of the spiritual life. Strive always to 'ring true.' The note of your spirit is sounded on the higher planes, and the knocks which you receive in your everyday life come to test whether you can really 'ring true.' To 'ring true' you must always sound *in tune* with the note of God which is within you.

The calm, faithful spirit which rings true throughout every experience of life, in both adversity and disappointment as well as in success, will gain admission into the heavenly places.

To find Truth

Seek always the tranquil way, my brother; cleanse your heart of all conflict, all fear; this you will do as you learn to understand the meaning of love.

A story is told of a neophyte who went into the wilderness to seek his Master. The Master kindly received him but told him that like all neophytes he must prove himself ready to advance on the path which led to spiritual enlightenment, illumination and power. The pupil was over-eager, and his mind over-active; he wanted power; he wanted to advance quickly on the spiritual path. But he lacked one essential

—complete love towards God and all mankind. He knew many things with his mind, but his heart was only slightly awake.

So his Master took him to the edge of a lake and firmly but gently led his pupil into its waters; he immersed and held him under the surface for a considerable time. When at last the pupil was allowed to rise, gasping and spluttering, and saying that it had been a terrible experience, the Master said, 'My son, when you long for God as desperately as you longed for air when you were under water, then you will find God; and in finding God, you will find all.'

Many believe in God; they know a great deal on the intellectual plane. They go through ceremonies and follow devious paths, hoping always to find God, but instead go round and round in circles and their hearts remain barren. It is one thing to know about esoteric truths, and quite another to become part of, to experience, actually to *live* them. The only sure way of entering the kingdom of heaven is through the heart, through love, through becoming at-one with God, who dwells within the silence of the heart. Aspiration towards God must become a yearning, a real driving force in you, until you feel ready to renounce everything that you think you possess, in order to become at-one with God. When you sincerely and truly long so much to love God and to know God's love that nothing else matters, then you will find Him, and all truth.

'Lead us not into Temptation'

My child, you have chosen to follow the spiritual path, and many, many times you have prayed: ' O God, do not desert me—do not let me fall— lead me not into temptation. Give me strength that I may not fail when the tempter speaks.' Nevertheless, you do fail; time and again the tempter with his worldliness triumphs over you, and you desert the path of Christ, the path of love.

Why does the soul have to endure these temptations? The answer is simple: without the temptations which life brings, the spirit of Christ in you could never develop and become strong. You would never acquire a clear vision so that you could see where you were going, but would continue to live, as so many do, in a state of vagueness and confusion.

Nearly every day, every hour and every minute of your daily life you are confronted by temptations which would divert you from the spiritual path; and you need constantly to gather strength to your spirit in order to resist the tempter, until the spirit of Christ grows strong within you. Perhaps you have never thought that all your daily temptations are bound up with the Law of Karma. For indeed 'whatsoever a man soweth, that shall he also reap.' This is both a divine and a natural law. As you sow and tend the seeds in your earth so will they grow. As you sow the seeds of thoughts, words and deeds, so will you have to reap the result of your sowing.

Do not, however, think that everything that comes to you is *bad* karma. On the contrary, every time you think lovingly, kindly and constructively, every time you help your brother man, you are sowing *good* karma which you cannot escape reaping, not only in the world to come, but in your present day of life.

Learning to become aware of the Presence of the Christ within you will do more than create pleasant spiritual experiences for you; it will also help you to build healthy soul-bodies, and as a result, healthy physical bodies for your future habitation during many lives to come. All the time you can be creating finer vehicles for yourself—physical, etheric, emotional, mental and celestial—to inhabit in future lives on earth or in higher spheres.

For many states of life are awaiting the child of God. You cannot see beauty if you are blind, or enjoy the perfume of a flower if you have no sense of smell; you cannot hear the music of the spheres if you are deaf. Therefore, you must develop those spiritual senses, those vehicles through which you, a divine soul, may experience and realise the glories of all those other spheres of life to which you are heir.

O my child, you are closed in clay, and cannot conceive the glories awaiting you when you have learnt to obey spiritual law by right living, right thinking and right action.

In fact what does this mean? Just this. Do not make excuses for yourself. Do not protest, 'I am only human, so what else can I do? How can I help failing?' No, you cannot help failing, but you can truly strive and earnestly pray that you may not fail again when in temptation. And if you keep pure in heart and hold fast to the simple love and faith of a little child, looking always to Christ the Son who is the human manifestation of God, and pray, 'Lord, be with me! I would be with Thee always,' then, my child, you will not fail.

The will in you to do right must be strong and enduring. You must have the will *to will the Will of God*. You must pray for strength to enable you to live as a child of God.

Forgiveness and Thankfulness

There are two qualities which a man must cherish in his heart if he would advance into the

Temple of that Star which led the Wise Men to Christ: these are forgiveness and thankfulness, simple qualities like keys which can open the gates to the mysteries of heaven. You cannot pass through the gates until you have mastered such simple human lessons.

Jesus said, 'Forgive us our trespasses as we forgive those who trespass against us.' Forgiveness is one of the hardest lessons that humanity has to learn; but as man forgives so he himself is forgiven. This is the law of forgiveness. It is not so difficult to forgive the big things; but we do not mean that kind of trespass; we have in mind the little things in life, the hasty judgments, the impatience with human frailties. We are all human and we all fail at times and need forgiveness. In the spirit world all have to be very forgiving. So will you also try to forgive those who err, who make mistakes largely because they do not understand? Forgive them also even if they do understand according to your knowledge. Forgiveness in your heart brings sunshine, peace of soul and tranquillity into your life. Forgive, therefore, not only the big debts, but trivial human frailties. When hasty emotions threaten to overwhelm you, just forgive. Then all shall be forgiven you, and God will bless you.

The second quality is thankfulness. Never

cease to feel thankful to God. This is the secret of a perfect life, for in the act of thanking God you become in tune with Him.

Thank God for all the blessings of your life, and for every opportunity offered to you during this incarnation which enables you to grow nearer to Christhood. Do not let your days slip by aimlessly, but be ever on the look-out for the meaning behind every episode which comes along. Life is not something just to be muddled through, but given so that you may welcome and rejoice in every experience; for these experiences are meant, not as a harsh chastisement or punishment, but as opportunities for you to learn to understand the wisdom of God's laws and the power of the spiritual light which emanates from God. Take with both hands that which the world would call bitterness, for within that bitterness you will find the nectar, the sweetness.

It is the way in which you accept your experiences that matters; the way you allow them to awaken the love of the Christ spirit in your heart.

Whatever ordeal lies before you, my child, remember the Christ presence, for it will never leave you, and it brings peace and courage. You may be deeply thankful for His love.

Did He not say, '*Lo! I am with you always*'?

II

The White Brotherhood

There are Masters of the Wisdom in both this world and in worlds beyond; they and even more evolved souls are formed into a vast brotherhood which is active in all planes of life, and is called the Great White Brotherhood. 'These are they which came out of great tribulation, and have washed their robes, and made them white in the blood of the Lamb.' They are always waiting in the silence to serve. If we could raise you to their level of thought or awareness, you would at once become conscious of their presence and power. They meditate and observe all things happening both in heaven and on earth; they become absorbed into Universal Mind, and are at-one with God.

In the process of man's soul-development he discards one by one the material veils which blind him to this vast array of spiritual power.

All that is good, true and beautiful on earth was begun, inspired and brought into manifestation under God by this true Brotherhood whose symbol is the Christ Star. Try to expand your consciousness and realise the immensity of the world-service undertaken by this Great White Brotherhood. The physical bodies which you inhabit are like little closed boxes; but by aspiration you can liberate yourself and become *en rapport* with this ancient and limitless Brotherhood beyond physical life.

So, when you feel distracted by material things, keep calm and still; remember the Brethren of the Silence, whose very power of achievement lies in this silence. If you can touch this silence, their power will flow into you and disperse all your fears.

The Love that guides your Life

The Elder Brethren seek above all to help their earthly brethren towards the great surrender to God. Nevertheless, it is no part of the work of the Brotherhood to make your path too easy, or to prevent you learning lessons, the mastery of which will gain for you an expansion of spiritual vision and consciousness. Be of good heart, keep simple in faith, be ready to surrender your cares and burdens to the spiritual love which watches over, guides and directs the child of Light.

We are able to bring you help when it is asked for selflessly. When the heart is filled with loving desire to serve humanity, help flows to you unhindered. By your love you set in motion certain helpful forces; your spirit sounds a clarion call in the heavens, and commands the creative forces of life which come flooding to you, much as the little corpuscles of the bloodstream rush to heal a wound when called upon to do so. All the forces of the Light rise up to help you when once you learn to call upon them in the right way. This is perfectly logical and scientific and can happen on all planes; but the aspirant has first to discipline himself on all planes of life before he can acquire power to command in spheres of spiritual activity. The mastery of himself can only come about as a result of continual, consistent practice of the Presence of God.

Become yourself a Centre of Love

The misunderstandings and conflicts which arise between people and nations shatter man's peace of mind and confidence in his future. But having a power of vision ranging beyond your mortal vision, we see a wonderful inner growth going on in man. Rays of light and love are being projected to the earth from the universal Star Brotherhood. You talk about love on your earth, but you have little understanding of the power and wonder of love as it exists and is practised on higher planes. This love, this light, this tenderness and understanding are all the time being poured out upon the earth to help mankind rise from darkness to light.

The one message which is always coming from the Brotherhood of the Star is of the necessity for man to learn to live as a centre of love and goodwill to all creatures. This is not an impossible task, but it requires constant attention and self-discipline.

There are many grades of humanity, and you cannot judge any one of them. All you can do is to become yourself a centre of love, recognising your own need for wider experience of human life, your need of training, of further development. For when you compare yourself with the Illuminati you will feel very humble— but so in turn do they.

Preserve a heart of love and compassion and keep your thoughts good, constructive and loving. You can render no greater service to God or man.

The Brethren are close

The silent Brothers are close to you in spirit; they know both the problems and the joys of your life, and understand the need of your soul.

Although you may suffer loneliness, you

are never truly alone; the companion of your spirit, your beloved, is with you all the time. You are only lonely if you isolate yourself in your physical life and consciousness. Your spirit can rise above this limitation and join your loved ones. But this means continual effort, an awakening of that inward knowing that you call 'faith.' You must have faith in God's love. At death there is physical separation, but no separation of the human spirit which is the real self. If you truly love your companion he is with you, closer than breathing, because you and he are both part of God.

Rise above the babble of the market-square, and abide in the quiet places of the spirit where you will hear the voices and know the companionship of the Shining Ones. If you can do this you will become a channel for the healing of men's souls and bodies.

Do not be anxious, or question your way; neither grow weary. Live in the Christ radiance and his power will sustain you. You will be guided by the Brethren in all you do. Accept and follow the Christ way.

III

Be Still

The way to discriminate between self-will and divine intuition is to learn first to rule the lower self and its stormy emotions and desires, for unruly emotions are a hindrance to the development of intuition. Turbulent water gives a broken reflection, or none at all; but when water is calm, clear and pure, there comes perfect reflection. In the same way, when the soul has trained itself to be still and peaceful, it truly reflects the spiritual worlds. This is intuition, an inward knowing.

Spirit messengers or angels are sent by God to help you, and will speak through your intuition. Do not shut them out, either through mental arrogance or for any other reason.

Be calm! Be still! Do one thing at a time quietly, tranquilly, and you will make the way clear in your soul for a greater inflowing · of spiritual power. As the Master comforted the disciples on the storm-tossed waters, so he will comfort you. The Water initiation is designed to bring control over the emotions. The Elder Brethren cannot work with you if your soul is like a turbulent sea. Lack of emotional control is the greatest hindrance in the service of the Master. Mental and soul peace—the achievement of controlled and wisely directed emotion —are essential to progress.

Where to look for Guidance

There come moments in your life when you feel wholly unable to deal with some material situation which arises; when you do not know what to do for the best, and are unable to make a decision. Some people like to take their troubles to the spirit friends and ask for guidance at such times. They feel that only a spirit being can really help them; but they fail to realise that it is not some spirit to whom they should turn for their help, but to the Spirit of God, the Great White Spirit whom they worship.

Christ said, 'Lo, I am with you always'— not only at certain times or during religious ceremonies, but always; for you are sons and daughters of the living God, and hold within your heart something of the nature and qualities of God.

That which your soul is seeking can be found within your own being. To find it, learn to be still and 'cast your burden upon the Lord.' In other words, let go, surrender, lay down your problems. Do not try to unravel the knot, which gets tighter and tighter the more you pull at it. Lay it down. Concentrate all your heart upon that gentle, loving personality, the Lord Jesus Christ, and all knots will be unloosed, all problems solved.

Now in your imagination behold the human form of the Lord Jesus; see him coming to you clothed in beauty, with hands outstretched to greet you. Feel his gentle, pure, sweet love radiating forth. . . . He comes, my child, to raise you above the turmoil of physical life into the peace of the spirit. He comes to help you that you may see a truer, purer vision of life; to discern the real from the unreal—which is your daily life on earth. He comes to set you free from burdens which are at times too heavy for you to carry alone.

Surrender yourself to this beautiful influence, and you will be comforted, healed and blest; frayed nerves will be soothed and comforted, and a joy unspeakable will unfold in your heart.

The Secret Place within the Heart

The purpose of man's life on this earth-planet is that he may demonstrate the spirit of the Son of God; that the beauty of the Christ life shall eventually manifest through matter. Man must learn to go reverently to the secret chamber of the heart and find there the Christ-man, the child of God. He must learn the inner secret of himself. We beg you not to devote too much attention to material things, but to seek first the secret of real creative power, deep, deep within, and behind all physical form.

Endeavour to find *yourself*, the real 'I' beneath the outer coats of flesh and mind which obscure it. To do this try to think in terms of three; first, think of the ordinary person that you are in daily life; next, think about the soul, known only to yourself (or so you think); and thirdly, try to find the place of stillness and quiet at the centre of your being, the real 'I.'

As you learn to withdraw into your inner self, the outer self will, as it were, dissolve; and the inner self begin to assert itself. This inner self is a personality, a soul—and a something more. If you will train yourself in contemplation, you will find that beneath the soul there is a place of stillness, of blankness, of nothingness if you like. Yet when you are confronted with the seeming nothingness which lies beneath the conscious self, you will gradually become aware of an all-ness, a sense of affinity with universal life and at-one-ment with God. In this condition there can be no separation, no darkness, no fear:

nothing exists but love and an exquisite joy which permeates your whole being.

Why then do you fear?

When we come down through the mists of the astral world into the still denser mists which envelop the earth, we feel and see how much suffering is caused through fear; indeed we see that the basis of most suffering is fear. We see the human mind largely dominated by fear of the future, fear of the unknown. Surely you know by now that whatever tangle you find yourself in, whatever emotional strain is yours, these cannot last for ever, but are passing phases which come only as lessons to teach you something of value? You are here that you may learn, may gain knowledge which is essential to your well-being; and it is the actual experience of living with your fellow man which brings you wisdom.

Wisdom also comes direct from heaven as the result of your reaching upward to heaven, to higher planes of heavenly understanding; and wisdom says that bitter and painful experiences grow yet more painful if you allow them to disturb you emotionally and mentally. The alternative is to learn to lay them aside, and in everything to depend upon the love of God.

Confusion will depart if you can contact

the Divine Heart by simple prayer uttered in faith and trust, and most of all in humility.

As the waves became still at the command of Jesus, so all your troubled emotions will be quieted when the Master takes possession of your heart.

So accept with love all that happens. Look for the lesson that has to be learnt from every experience, bad or good. Look up to God daily, hourly, and be filled with the divine light and love. It pours like a golden ray into your heart and head centres, cleansing, healing, uplifting, steadying, giving you control over all your weakness.

The deep Silence where is Love

Brethren, from the Centre of all life, from the place of deep Silence where all is love, we bring you peace. If you will withdraw from the thraldom of your physical existence and seek the Source of all life, you will find a deep peace that nothing can disturb. By the divine will within, withdraw from the outermost and seek peace and truth at the Centre of all life. Although storms may rage on the outer plane, this deep inner peace is the source of all your strength; from that Centre you draw the sustenance and guidance you need at all times.

Peace is a dynamic power. From the heart of peace comes right action. When men think and act in haste, conflict and pain usually result. So, in your own daily lives, strive for inner tranquillity. Right action will then be yours. Having acted rightly, patiently wait for the outworking of the will of God.

Learn to be still. When in doubt do nothing. Be constant, and rest in the consciousness of the Eternal Love and Wisdom. . . .

Turn, my child, to the Source of all life, and allow the divine power within to rise up and direct you. This power comes in fulness when you touch that deep peace which is truth, which is God. . . . Now you feel your burdens slipping away. There are no burdens, my child . . . only those you make for yourself to bear—and all of you do this.

God's peace we leave with you. Be ready at all times to accept His will, to accept the way which opens before you, knowing there is no other; then meekly follow that path and trust in the Great Spirit.

The Eternal Presence

The Presence of the Lord Christ should become very real to you. No human soul need ever live removed from this companionship, for

Christ does not exclude or withdraw Himself from anyone. But you must separate yourself from worldly thoughts and desires before you can become aware of His presence.

Those of you whose duty and work take you among conditions of harsh worldliness will find it difficult to keep attuned to the eternal spirit of peace and love. But remember, my child, that you should at all times keep in your heart the thought of the presence of Christ. Remember also that Christ, when manifesting through Jesus of Nazareth, was ever peaceful and calm amidst the turmoil of worldliness.

His disciples must seek to find this quietude and sweetness in the midst of the crowd. It is easier in solitude to keep close to him; but the tried, the happy and the great man is he who keeps aware of his Master, despite the pressure of the multitude. Strive, therefore, even in the midst of turmoil to hold true communion with your Master. Nothing, except your own thoughts and feelings, can separate you from him and from the Centre of Light.

Another valuable lesson which you as the pupil of the Master have to learn is that of patience—patience when you are confronted with material difficulties; patience to know that all is in God's hands, and will work out for good, for God. Bear patiently your difficulties and problems, knowing that God, all Love and all Wisdom, holds you and all humanity within His heart.

If you would be happy and give greater happiness to all whom you contact, seek those quiet places of the spirit; seek to discriminate between the unreal, which is of the world, and the reality, which is of the spirit.

IV

Acceptance

Men are careless and heedless with their thoughts, secure in the belief that they can hide them from their companions. But in the realms of spirit there is no cloaking of thought. All is thrown open; all thoughts are known. Would that it could be so on earth! If men and women only knew that their thoughts could be seen and heard by others, even as their physical forms are seen and heard, they would quickly learn to control them.

The Master looks into the heart of the aspirant, for he knows that what he sees in the heart will be expressed in the thought, and what is expressed in the thought will take form on the physical plane. So guard well your thoughts, keep them pure in the love of God. Ever seek the true interpretation of all that you see and hear. Continually make an effort to live according to spiritual values, refusing to be entangled and held down by false conceptions. When you see the right, firmly hold to the right and do the right, uninfluenced by material conditions or consequences. The spiritual law is such that it will never lead you astray. Follow it truly and you cannot go wrong; but you must have courage to hold fast to any decision you may make.

Look up to the Golden One . . . absorb into your being His golden rays. . . . His strength shall be given to you.

'Thy Will be done'

Do not look primarily for physical or material results arising out of your endeavours, but for the stirring of pure spirit. Learn to discriminate between the real and the unreal. For it must become a natural and spontaneous reaction for you to see beneath material happenings and recognise the life of Christ at work. The Christ way of life is the only reality.

You cannot make demands upon God either verbally or mentally; but you can most surely earn God's blessing and help by living according to His spiritual laws as they are one by one revealed to you. As soon as the aspirant begins to live the true inner life of a Son of God, he sounds a note which echoes throughout the spiritual universe like a great mantram or word of power, and in consequence his life, without his making any mental demands, draws to itself all the good things which the loving Father wishes to bestow upon it.

If you feel disappointed because what you want does not appear, we tell you in all sincerity and love that this is because you have yet to fulfil the requirements of God. But take heart; keep on striving, keep on living from your heart as the Christ taught you to live, until it becomes as natural to you as breathing. Then you will no longer hold back the blessings on all planes of life which are even now waiting for you.

If you are tempted to make demands upon God or the spiritual powers you may have cause to regret it; because such demands, although they may be granted, may result in your own discomfiture, pain and suffering. The true way, the only way is to surrender to the will and the love of God saying, 'Thy will be done in earth'—in this earthly tabernacle which is myself—'as it is being done in heaven'—in that state of perfect happiness, harmony, love, where all blessings flow without hindrance from the Heart of Love to all Thy children.

Learn discernment and discrimination in prayer as in all else. And the blessing of all-love be upon you!

Wait upon God

You, in whom love and desire to help humanity have been awakened, are so eager that you sometimes try to rush forward on the path. But remember, you cannot rush God, and you cannot push past God. If you try to rush forward too quickly you will come up against a 'sharp instrument' which will arrest you, perhaps painfully. Therefore be patient and learn to wait upon God. Your Bible tells you that there is an acceptable time of the Lord. There is an acceptable time for everything; this is spiritual law.

The way of God is slow and sure; there is a time for action and a time for silence and inaction. When you must needs wait during one of these periods of inaction, be patient, faithful, and trusting. You will in time receive a fuller reward than you can possibly foresee or imagine; a reward 'pressed down and running over' that will be your joy, not so much because of outer happenings which please you, but mainly because a change has taken place within your inner self, which has brought a joy not understood by the worldly man, a peace beyond all worldly understanding.

The Source of all Strength

Cease to think in terms of earth. Do not allow your thoughts to limit your life, or the life-force which continually flows into you. You limit this power by negative thoughts, but its flow increases in you and in your life when you attune your thoughts to the 'Star' which is the Christ. There is much activity in your world; your life on the earth plane is over-burdened with activity; but you must learn to become aware of the inner life, the plane of spirit deep within you. You are creating all the time; every moment of your life you are creating your inner world to which you will withdraw when your physical body has ceased its functioning.

As you give yourselves in service, so is your life-force being replenished. All the strength that you need in your service to the outer life is flowing into you from the spiritual state. Did not Jesus tell you to take no thought for the morrow, that all your needs would be supplied? 'Consider the lilies of the field, how they grow; they toil not, neither do they spin: and yet I say unto you, that even Solomon in all his glory was not arrayed like one of these.'

There is so much confusion of thought, so much turmoil all round you in the world, that you need help to give you more confidence and strength of purpose. *In silence shall be your strength.*

Creation, not Destruction

The thought of Christ must become real; the living image of the Christ life be ever present in your heart. You must refuse to see evil and destruction. You must live creating beauty in your mind as God created beauty in His mind. Your thoughts should always be positive because your mind-images will in the course of time register themselves on other minds; and also because that which you think today, you will yourself become tomorrow. Your body in its well- or ill-being will reproduce your thoughts. This is spiritual and scientific law. If you would have a better world, start to create it for yourself, now, at this very instant in your mind; hold the positive thought continually; refuse to allow any other thought to banish it from your consciousness. Then raise your whole vibration and your aspiration to your Creator, praying, 'Breathe on me, Breath of God. . . .'

God breathed into Adam the breath of life; and God will breathe into you this same breath of life if you will hold the thought of this perfect life in your mind and heart. Then you will be able to say in truth, as the Master Jesus did, 'The Father and I are one. . . .' 'I am in the Father and the Father in me.' Hold fast to this realisation of the Light, of the Life *within* you. Let the Light manifest through you, let it shine throughout the world!

You as an individual are of the greatest importance, because the perfect expression of

God through you can influence countless lives. Every human soul is of the utmost importance because every soul is potentially a reflector of God's life.

You can best help humanity towards brotherhood by seeking wisdom, prompted by the love in your heart; by learning to withhold criticism and condemnation; by seeing only the God struggling for manifestation in man. Be on the alert to obey the Voice within your heart; hold fast to courage and a deep faith that the Light can never be extinguished. All else may fail but the Light—Christ the Son—will endure.

May the God of love bless you now, and breathe into your waiting hearts the breath of Life. . . .

New Birth

The familiar story of the birth of Jesus in Bethlehem, in the stable with only animals for companions, also describes in symbolic form the birth of the Light, or the Christ-Child, in a human heart reduced to lowliness and humility through sorrow, and through spiritual and often through material need. When thus reduced the soul is called to take shelter in a simple stable or cave. The cave is the heart of man wherein the Christ light comes to birth. When all arrogance and fear have departed and man gives himself simply and completely to God, the birth of the Christ-Child takes place in him.

When you are suffering the pangs of this birth, and you feel lonely and dissatisfied and tempted to question the love of God; when the sore questions 'Why?' 'Why?' 'Why?' remain unanswered; try to remember that there *is* a solid reason for everything that happens in your life, and accept with patience and humility all that comes. For the pain, the disappointment and loneliness come to help you bring to birth and full stature the beautiful spirit of the Son of God in your heart, a happening which will bless you beyond all your dreams.

V

The Transforming Power

You become anxious about your earthly problems because you are depending solely upon yourself, forgetting the limitless power upon which you may draw. Very simply we would advise you to do your best according to your opportunities in earthly life. You may then safely leave the working out of the plan to the Great White Spirit and to the servers and messengers who come to help individuals as well as groups and nations. If you would follow this rule, and act and think and speak rightly according to the spiritual law which you are beginning to understand, you need never fear the future. For God is love and wisdom, and by the operation of His divine law good cometh out of so-called evil. Indeed good comes: it is the natural product of the seeds of goodwill, of the application of the law of love to man's affairs. Do your best with the material God has given you, and keep your vision for ever on the Perfect One, the Perfect Life. You will then be putting the law into operation, and you will gradually see results, working out not in your way perhaps, but more beautiful and more perfect in completion than you had ever conceived and hoped for.

The secrets of the universe are contained within the Light, and for this reason there will be a release of the secrets of nature to those who seek first the kingdom of God. Be untiring in your work but depend not upon your own strength. That would bring you limitation. Look to the Great Spirit, the White Spirit, for all your needs and for the release of that inner strength within you. Be undaunted, be untiring, but depend not upon yourself. Look to the infinite love and glory of the Son, Christ.

The Fountain of Life

Within you is the golden light of the Sun, and only you can release this radiation from within your own centre. Try to realise that within your heart-centre is the same blazing, golden sun as the one you contemplate in your aspirations, and that this infinite source of power is within your own being.

The great Light of the Sun floods you with His glory and His life, and by your devotion to the Christ light and the personality of the Lord Christ you will open yourself to the incoming of the Sun, which will flood your being and stimulate and release the divine fire within yourself.

You could be as kings, ruling supreme over all negative conditions in your lives; but too often you succumb to the negative forces instead of releasing, with your own master key, the power and light stored up within you to combat these forces. The only way to make use of this key is by constant and continuous practice of awareness of the presence of this glorious Light within you and around you.

So, whenever you feel depressed and life seems a burden to you, break the bondage of your thought to find the fountain of life within your being; feel within your breast the power which is there. The Great White Spirit—the golden Sun, the Source of all life—will not fail to raise you up if you will only allow yourself to be raised. You all keep yourselves in bondage, in chains! Throw off the chains of earthly darkness and see yourselves as you truly are, sons and daughters of the blazing, golden light of the Sun of God.

In the beginning Men from the Sun came to earth to teach mankind the way of life; and the radiation from the hearts of these Sun-men of long ago was such that even the human form grew to a great size under its influence.

If you could see with clear vision the radiation of a great one or Master you would behold a golden and rainbow light reaching far beyond the small human figure outlined at its centre. Each one of you is potentially a Sun-man. You too can use your will, your love, your prayers to radiate this light to your fellows. As Jesus said, 'And I, if I be lifted up'—from the earth—'will draw all men unto me.'

This is the right way to overcome all evil, to overcome cruelty, conflict and war. Only you must become very certain in your knowledge that the light of the Sun will absorb into itself and consume all darkness.

Desirelessness

One of the lessons all souls have to learn is the lesson of love. Personal love of a selfless nature is beautiful and it makes life lovely and brings great happiness. But the personal love must be broad and wide. Love, like power, must be poised; it must be steady; it must in a sense be impersonal. You may think that impersonal love is cold, but this is not so. Impersonal love is pure and without condemnation; it is all-embracing, all-enfolding, all tenderness. Above all, it is love without pain.

If your love has brought you pain, there is something wrong with it. Learn to love, then, without pain, and you will have learnt the main lesson love has to teach. Is it hard? Yes, to you on earth all these things seem hard, but that rich reward which follows the learning of the lesson on earth is worth the struggle.

'Thou shalt love the Lord thy God with all thy heart, with all thy soul and with all thy mind; and thy neighbour as thyself. Upon these two commandments hangs all the law.' Love thy neighbour, love thy God. All selfish desire, all desire to have and to hold must go; you must be prepared to lose, to give—all. This does not mean that all will of necessity be demanded of you, but rather that desire for possession must fall away. You must so centre your love upon the Christ spirit that you long only to become more aware of His radiance, peace, strength. But to enter into and share His great light you must encompass all living creatures with your love. In Him there is no separation from any living thing; yet in Him is liberation.

Strive also to become more worthy of the Master's love. Outer circumstances do not matter. Be human, be happy, be ready to enjoy all the beauties of the earthly life, make proper use of all God's gifts, but do not abuse them—or abuse yourself—by misuse. Above all, guard well the inner sanctuary of your soul, remembering each morning when you rise that the happenings of the coming day are prepared for you by God's laws; and that all that will matter is your

personal reaction to what the day will bring.
Be still within and know God.

The Essence of Divine Love

There is no power greater than the Christ light.
Control and command over the physical and
spiritual atoms are achieved not by power of
man's earthly mind but by the very essence of
the lowly spirit of the gentle Christ.

Whatever problem lies before you can be
solved by the Christ love, the great and only true
solvent of all problems. The life, the power of
the Christ spirit can never be destroyed. Man's
body may die, people disappoint him, and his
world may pass away, but the spirit of the Son
of God can never fail. His light is life. Live in
this light forever!

We understand how easily weariness of
mind and body can possess you, for we ourselves
have not forgotten our earthly experiences. We
understand the heaviness of matter, and how it
weighs you down. Yet saints and sages have
evolved bodies that have become so light and
vibrant that they live and move between the
physical and etheric state. This same process of
evolution is continually going on in all physical
matter; all humanity is progressing upwards in
its return to the divine Father-Mother God, and

in the process is shedding both the denser atoms and appetites of the lower man. In the degree this happens, so does the vibration of Mother Earth herself quicken and her substance become less gross.

If you will meditate upon the presence of the beautiful Christ spirit you will absorb the essence of His Being; the essence or perfume which will quicken your own bodily vibration so that all tiredness and heaviness depart. You will not know tiredness when you come to the edge of the aura of the Great One. We can only tell you about these things. They wait for you to experience them for yourself.

Do you remember the wonderful healings which took place when the crowds pressed round the beloved Master? To be near him, to touch his holy aura was sufficient to revitalise the soul of the sick man who sought healing.

Again we say that the one truth, the one power the world is waiting for, is the power of the pure and holy Christ spirit. To you the world may appear to be in chaos, but we assure you that out of chaos and suffering a better understanding is coming to birth. Would that we could find words to convince you of this truth; but since words cannot of themselves always bring conviction, we can only endeavour to impart to you the essence of divine love.

The way to work for the Great White Brotherhood is always by love, and never by force in any shape or form. No man must force his own individual or personal views on other men. To love them is the only way to win them.

In Love there is no Separation

Think of yourself as being held within that Light which is the heart of all creation, which manifests as Love. In this consciousness there is no separation between loved ones after death *because there is no death.* The soul cannot die.

On earth, with its many distractions on the physical plane, you can become cut off from that power; but you are in the physical life in order to gain spiritual strength, and for no other purpose; you are here to gain spiritual or God-consciousness, and to disentangle your human consciousness from the ignorance and the mists of the physical life. The material world with all its harshness and greed brings sickness and unhappiness and fear to the soul. But when you can disentangle yourself from the cares and trivialities of your outer environment you are happy and at peace.

We want you to become each day more aware of the reality of the unseen worlds, of the presence of the unseen. We would emphasise the truth of the saying, 'In spirit there is no separation'; but first you must understand what is meant by the word 'spirit.' Spirit is the God-consciousness within man. Within yourself is that wonderful love of God, and as you love in simplicity of heart you are becoming God-conscious, you are becoming conscious of the one-ness of spirit. As soon as you truly love, you are in touch with the Infinite. Because you are in touch with the Infinite, you are conscious of all love, and there is no longer separation between this world and the next. All power is yours because you have reached at-one-ment. Then you can truly say, as did the Master of Masters, 'I and the Father are one.'

The Breath of God

Breathe in the Holy Breath, the perfect breath of life. Breathe out the blessing of love. Practise this rhythm of holy breathing, breathing in the life of the Creator. Let it flow through your whole being, harmonising, adjusting, purifying, ennobling your whole life. Your Father in heaven knows your thoughts, your prayers, your strength and your weakness, and He has one thought for you; it is that you should realise His love for you. He does not want you to suffer or to be unhappy; He wants you to be at peace because you know Him and His power. Do not think of God as a Universal Power without intelligence or love or personality. God still takes form and comes among you, and you must look for Him in form everywhere in your life. Seek and ye shall find. He comes to you specially in the forms of the Illumined Ones, the Elder Brethren, and in the form of the Golden One. He has created you, man, in His own image, and possessed of infinite possibilities. ' Be ye perfect as your Father in heaven is perfect.' Say to yourself every morning: 'I am perfect as my Father created me perfect. I am divine love. I am divine peace.' When you go to sleep at night let your last thought be of praise and thankfulness to God. Think of crossing the river to the world of light. Let the divine will within you be your director both in sleep and waking. Do not look about you on the earth plane for inharmony and for those who hurt you and who are rough and unkind. Look above them. Keep your thoughts always fixed upon the good, the true and the beautiful God-life. Breathe in the breath of God. Breathe out the blessing of love and healing upon the earth. You, the child of God, are whole, you are holy, and as you truly and earnestly think, so you become.

Let all frets and fears and inharmonies fall behind you and live tranquilly in His life.

The Resurrection and the Life

The Master, Jesus the Christ, understood human frailty and knew the power of man's earthly mind to separate him from his true inheritance.

Could you only remain firm in the realisation of indwelling spiritual life and power, you could be instantly healed of all disability. We know the pull of the physical body and how the earthly mind dominates you; nevertheless, again and again we say, 'Seek ye first the kingdom of God and all these things shall be added unto you.' By strenuous effort, through prayer, devotion and adoration, you can rise above the downward pull of the earthly mind. Then dwell for a while in meditation with the radiant ones, the Great White Brotherhood invisible, for these are they who have passed through great tribulation and whose raiment is now whiter than snow. And this means that they are cleansed from all impurity, they have triumphed over the earth.

However difficult your pathway may seem to you, daily seek the glory of the God-life. To do so, close down the senses of earth and soar in your higher mind (or in what you call your imagination) into Christ's sphere of glory and power, and know that this power and light is your real life; it is the re-creative force which can constantly flow through you, causing every ill to fade from your body. At least you can reach that pinnacle of perfection, wholeness and holiness. Later, the ills of the body *may* reassert themselves. Yet do not become despondent; the more frequently you reach that height of spiritual consciousness, the more surely and quickly will every sickness become healed. When Jesus said, 'I am the resurrection and the life,' he did not mean that only in him was resurrection and life, but in every one of God's children. For the life of God is latent within you; and it will also flow into you from the great heavenly hosts. You too can learn to say with all the strength of your spirit, 'I am the resurrection and the life!' Then that life-force stirs and rises within, and your spirit shines like a jewel in its casket. 'I AM the way. I AM the truth. I AM the life.' When uttering these words Jesus did not speak of his human or personal self. It was the Christ within him which spoke those words of truth.

We come only to help you to rise above disappointment, fear and all poverty of life. The way to rise is quite clear. . . . It is by prayer, adoration and love. The heart of the golden Sun of God is the source of your spiritual strength.

VI

The Triumph of Love

It is well for us all to recognise the existence of a law which ensures perfect justice for every human life, a balancing of pain with joy. A soul who suffers apparent injustice may by its reaction learn vital truths. There is always joy to come corresponding to any measure of suffering endured rightly. If there is seeming loss, remember God never takes away without giving. You will say, 'But God can never give back to me the loved one whom death has taken away!' My child, God is already offering you a gift which will perhaps eventually prove even more precious both to you and your loved one. To obtain this gift you must first surrender your will to His, and recognise that a divine justice permeates all the happenings of human life. Opportunity has been given to you to open your heart to the warm, radiant love of the Divine. It may be that your sorrow and loss will enable you at last to find God.

Beloved, put out your hand to grasp the hand of God. . . . Be not afraid. . . . He will lead you onward step by step. Make a steadfast effort to walk His way and you will pass all your tests and initiations.

Peace of heart bless you! You are not alone, remember. Age-old companions of your spirit are walking by your side. You are indeed encompassed by a cloud of unseen radiant companions on your way. In love there can be no separation. In God's life alone you can fully live and know a supreme happiness beyond all earthly understanding.

The Great Initiation

The Christ spirit glorifies and blesses you, and triumphs with you over the darkness and sorrow of earthly life.

The crucifixion of Jesus was an experience which awaits every human soul during its path of evolution—is indeed one which you may even now be passing through in your inner self, for crucifixion can take many forms.

May it comfort you to know that everyone who undergoes some experience which might be described as a crucifixion, involving pain or soul-anguish, is not only gaining wisdom and truth in himself but is also doing something valuable for the whole of humanity. For anyone who can meet such testings of the soul with the same resolution and tranquillity that Jesus showed is quickening the vibrations of the whole earth.

All that the Master Jesus suffered during his crucifixion was endured in a spirit of perfect love. This is the very heart of the spiritual meaning of the Earth initiation, or crucifixion. Jesus demonstrated great love in his treatment of his betrayer, Judas. All of us have a share of the Judas nature in us, which on occasion denies and betrays our Lord, the Christ spirit within us. But there is another interpretation of this story. When karma exists between two souls the one who is wronged should forgive the debtor. Too often there is retaliation instead, and the debt is tossed backwards and forwards between the two, perhaps through several lives, so that both suffer. On this occasion Jesus forgave Judas and relieved him of his karmic debt.

In the garden of Gethsemane Jesus, you will recall, also healed the soldier wounded by Peter's sword. The whole story of the crucifixion demonstrates, as incident follows incident, not only the great love of the Master, but above all how vital it is for the soul when undergoing initiation to meet all trials, hardships and bitterness without anger or resentment, and in a spirit of true and perfect love. This is where so many fall short in their attitude towards the difficulties of everyday life. The lower self is full of pride and resents having to surrender to the will of the Father; and so long as it resents, it has to suffer. But when once the heart bows down in acceptance of the wisdom of God's plan, then there is no suffering. You make real progress and are filled with a peace which the world cannot give.

The crucifixion of the soul means, in essence, the surrender of the lower self; when all has been surrendered to God, the soul, having been thoroughly tried, tested and not found wanting, takes the path of Mastership.

The Rose upon the Cross

Beloved brother, try to visualise, as you read these words, a delicate pink rose, perfect in form and colour, opening its petals to the spiritual sun which falls upon it. Try to become *en rapport* with that rose . . . inhale the spiritual perfume, absorb the delicacy of its life, its aura. . . . It will raise you far above the earth into a world of silence, peace, love, and truth. . . .

This rose is the symbol of the Christ-life, the Christ-sweetness and purity, of life untainted by the earth. We know of no symbol so perfect as this to convey to the mind the love of the Christ spirit. Nor is there any symbol which so perfectly illustrates the cosmic truth of

Eastertime, for Easter is a time of sweet surrender to the Christ spirit.

'May the rose bloom upon your cross!' This was the old wish for the aspirant on the path. In other words it meant that through constant striving towards the Light he might transmute the heavy cross of matter (his earthly self) into the fragrant Rose of the spiritual life. This is known in the White Brotherhood as the Earth initiation, when the soul, having seen the glory of the Father, is able to demonstrate that glory in its actions on earth. It is one thing to know theoretically but practice is very far from theory. The Earth initiation means putting into practice the Christ spirit.

The soul passes that degree when it can lay aside all the claims and desires of the earthly life, and can *at will* go direct to the heart of Christ. Do you think that this is beyond your power? We assure you that it is not. You may not yet be ready fully to pass the Earth initiation, but you are coming nearer to doing so every time you surrender your own will or sacrifice some dear desire. Every time you can feel your whole being filled with the love of Christ, and you *live* that love for your brother man, you are to a certain degree attaining mastery over the body of earth.

The whole life of Jesus demonstrated how mortal man can be glorified by the indwelling

Christ spirit. Man's purpose here is that the Christ shall glorify him and through him glorify the whole earth, shall quicken the vibrations of earthly matter until the whole planet becomes etherealised and spiritualised.

So think not of the crucified but of the arisen Christ with outstretched arms glorious in the heart of the blazing sun. He comes as a promise of what lies before man's own soul, a promise that you also will arise to the full stature of manhood and Christhood.

Use your inner vision, your imagination, and look if you can upon that lovely face, tender, understanding, kind and loving. His aura embraces you. Underneath you are the everlasting arms of this all-pervading spirit of love. Nothing can harm you. Whatever lies before you is wholly good.

He is bringing the symbols of the wheat and the grape. He offers you the bread of life. 'Take, eat my bread, the bread which comes to you from heaven.' Accept and eat the bread of life. . . . Accept your daily karma for this is the bread which feeds your soul.

He offers you the juice of the grape, the essence of His spirit, the essence of divine love. Drink from the cup that your heart may be filled with love, for love is the fulfilling of the law and through love man is made whole.